Afghan Crochet Tutorials

Traditional Afghan Patterns and Guide for Beginners

Copyright © 2023

All rights reserved.

DEDICATION

The author and publisher have provided this e-book to you for your personal use only. You may not make this e-book publicly available in any way. Copyright infringement is against the law. If you believe the copy of this e-book you are reading infringes on the author's copyright, please notify the publisher at: https://us.macmillan.com/piracy

Afghan Crochet Tutorials

Contents

Sophie's Garden Crochet Blanket 1

Rainbow Tunisian Entrelac Crochet Blanket 5

Lacy Shell Afghan 15

Crochet One to Two Skein Throw 20

Arrow Stitch Afghan 23

Ferris Wheel Baby Blanket 26

Crocheted Cuddly Kittens Afghan 29

Princess Crocodile Stitch Baby Blanket 33

Rainbow Delight Baby Afghan 38

The Coziest Crocheted Baby Blanket Ever 40

Rose Twists Afghan 42

Snowflake Afghan 45

Shades of Amber Tunisian Afghan 48

White Hibiscus Hexagon Afghan 53

Blue Heirloom Afghan 57

Colonial Charm Afghan 59

Afghan Crochet Tutorials

Sophie's Garden Crochet Blanket

Gauge

Using worsted weight yarn and dc stitches:

8 rows and 18 st's per 4" (10 cm) square.

Size

Afghan Crochet Tutorials

19" (48 cm) in diameter.

Materials

4 mm crochet hook (US G/6 UK 8)

Worsted weight yarn or double knit yarn (light worsted weight) – approx. 450 meters/500 yards

Yarn Needle

Different sizes

Using a gauge of 7 rows and 16 st's per 4" (10 cm) square, your final size will be roughly 22" (56 cm). I get this gauge by using a 5.5 mm crochet hook (US 9/I UK 5) and worsted weight yarn.

Using a gauge of 6 rows and 14 st's per 4" (10 cm) square, your final size will be roughly 24" (61 cm). I get this gauge by using bulky yarn and a 6 mm crochet hook (US 10/J UK 4) OR 2 strands of double knit yarn and a 5.5 mm crochet hook (US 9/I UK 5).

Afghan Crochet Tutorials

Instructions

Update 2/3/15: Sophie's Garden is now growing into Sophie's Universe. I have removed the photo tutorial that used to live here and I have added links to the new and improved tutorials. The instructions remain the same, so if you were in the middle of a round, just hop over to the new tutorial and continue on.

Sophie's Garden Pattern/Tutorials

Part 1: The instructions for Rounds 1 – 8 can be found HERE as Part 1 of Sophie's Universe.

Part 2: The instructions for Rounds 9 – 15 can be found HERE as Part 2 of Sophie's Universe.

Part 3: The instructions for Rounds 16 – 25 can be found HERE as Part 3 of Sophie's Universe.

Part 4: The instructions for Rounds 26 – 36 can be found HERE as Part 4 of Sophie's Universe.

Afghan Crochet Tutorials

Rainbow Tunisian Entrelac Crochet Blanket

MEASUREMENTS Approx 35" x 42" [89 x 106.5 cm].

GAUGE 9 sts and 10 rows = 4" [10 cm].

Afghan Crochet Tutorials

Materials

Bernat® Softee Baby Chunky™ (5 oz/142 g; 155 yds/142 m)

Contrast A Candy Apple Red (96008); 1 ball

Contrast B Creamsicle (96013); 1 ball

Contrast C Buttercup (96014); 1 ball

Contrast D Sprout Green (96010); 1 ball

Contrast E Dragon Green (96009); 1 ball

Contrast F Blue Lagoon (96011); 1 ball

Contrast G Indigo (96015); 1 ball

Contrast H Grape (96012); 1 ball

Size U.S. M/13 (9 mm) flexible cable Tunisian crochet hook or size needed to obtain gauge.

Afghan Crochet Tutorials

Forward Pass

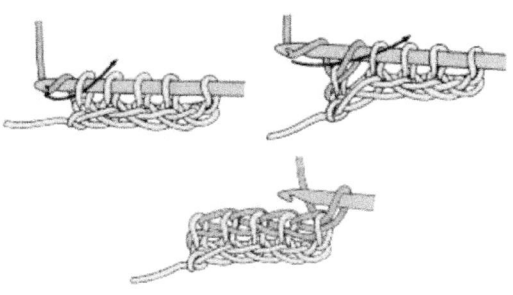

Return Pass

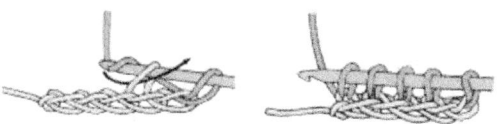

Tunisian Simple Stitch (Tss)

1. Insert hook from right to left behind single vertical thread.
2. Yoh
3. Draw loop through and leave on hook.

Afghan Crochet Tutorials

Abbreviations

Alt = Alternate

Approx = Approximately

Beg = Beginning

Ch = Chain(s)

Cont = Continue(ity)

Pat = Pattern

Rem = Remain(ing)

Rep = Repeat

RS = Right side

Sc = Single crochet

Sl st = Slip stitch

Sp = Space(s)

St(s) = Stitch(es)

Tss = Tunisian simple stitch

Yoh = Yarn over hook

Stripe Pat:

Afghan Crochet Tutorials

Work 1 Strip of each color: A, B, C, D, E, F, G and H. These 8 rows form Stripe Pat.

Notes: Work all rows with RS of work facing. To draw up a loop through single vertical bar or front bar of first st, always insert hook from right to left. For easier count of side sts, do not work Ch 1 at beg and end of every row.

Instructions

FIRST STRIP (worked with A)

With A, ch 112.

First Triangle

1st row: Work 1 regular sc in 2nd ch from hook. Do not turn.

2nd row: Forward pass: (Right to left). Draw up a loop through front bar of first st. Draw up a loop in next ch. 3 loops on hook. Do not turn.

Return pass: (Left to right). (Yoh and draw through 2 loops on hook) twice. 1 loop rem on hook. Do not turn.

3rd row: Forward pass: (Right to left). Tss in each of first 2 sts. Draw up a loop in next ch. 4 loops on hook. Do not turn.

Return pass: (Left to right). (Yoh and draw through 2 loops on hook) 3 times. 1 loop rem on hook. Do not turn.

4th row: Forward pass: (Right to left). Tss in each of first 3 sts. Draw up a loop in next ch. 5 loops on hook. Do not turn.

Return pass: (Left to right). (Yoh and draw through 2 loops on hook) 4 times. 1 loop rem on hook. Do not turn.

5th row: Forward pass: (Right to left). Tss in each of first 4 sts. Draw up a loop in next ch. 6 loops on hook. Do not turn.

Return pass: (Left to right). (Yoh and draw through 2 loops on hook) 5 times. 1 loop rem on hook. Do not turn.

6th row: Forward pass: (Right to left). Tss in each of first 5 sts. Draw up a loop in next ch. 7 loops on hook. Do not turn.

Return pass: (Left to right). (Yoh and draw through 2 loops on hook) 6 times. 1 loop rem on hook. Do not turn.

7th row: Sl st loosely in each of next 5 single vertical bars. Sl st in same sp as last st worked. First Triangle complete. 1 loop rem on hook.

First Square:

**1st row: Forward pass: (Right to left). Draw up a loop in each of next 6 ch and leave on hook. 7 loops on hook. Do not turn.

Return pass for all rows: (Left to right). *Yoh and draw through 2 loops on hook. Rep from * until 1 loop rem on hook. Do not turn.

2nd to 5th rows: Forward pass: (Right to left). Tss in each of first 5 sts. Draw up a loop in next ch. Do not turn.

Afghan Crochet Tutorials

Rep, then Return pass once.

Next row: Sl st loosely into each of next 5 single vertical bars. Sl st in last worked ch.** First Square complete.

Second to Ninth Squares: Work from ** to ** as given for First Square.

Last Triangle

1st row: Forward pass: (Right to left). Draw up a loop in each of next 6 ch and leave on hook. 7 loops on hook. Do not turn.

Return pass for all rows: (Left to right). *Yoh and draw through 2 loops on hook. Rep from * until 1 loop rem on hook. Do not turn.

2nd row: Forward pass: (Right to left). Tss in each of first 5 sts. Do not turn.

3rd row: Forward pass: (Right to left). Tss in each of first 4 sts. Do not turn.

4th row: Forward pass: (Right to left). Tss in each of first 3 sts. Do not turn.

5th row: Forward pass: (Right to left). Tss in each of first 2 sts. Do not turn.

6th row: Forward pass: (Right to left). Tss in first st. Do not turn.

Return pass: (Left to right). Yoh and draw through 2 loops on hook. 1 loop rem on hook. Fasten off.

Afghan Crochet Tutorials

SECOND STRIP (worked with B)

First Square

With RS facing, join B with sl st at top corner of First Triangle.

***1st row: Forward pass: (Right to left). Working through both loops of sl sts, draw up a loop in each of next 6 sl sts and leave on hook. 7 loops on hook. Do not turn.

Return pass for all rows:(Left to right). *Yoh and draw through 2 loops on hook. Rep from * until 1 loop rem on hook. Do not turn.

2nd to 5th rows: Forward pass: (Right to left). Tss in each of first 5 sts. Draw up a loop in next st of next Square. Do not turn.

Rep, then Return pass once.

Next row: Sl st loosely into each of next 5 single vertical bars. Sl st in top of square of 1st Strip.*** First Square complete.

Second to Eighth Squares: Rep from *** to *** as given for First Square of Second Strip. Fasten off at end of last Square.

THIRD STRIP (worked with C)

First Triangle

With RS facing, join C with sl st to same sp where First Square of previous row started.

1st row: Forward pass: (Right to left). Ch 1. 1 sc in same sp as sl st. Draw up a loop through front vertical bar of first sc. Draw up a loop

Afghan Crochet Tutorials

in first st of First Square of Second Strip and leave on hook. 3 loops on hook.

Return pass: (Left to right). (Yoh and draw through 2 loops on hook) twice. 1 loop rem on hook. Do not turn.

2nd row: Forward pass: (Right to left). Tss in each of first 2 sts. Tss in single vertical bar of next Square. 4 loops on hook. Do not turn.

Return pass: (Left to right). (Yoh and draw through 2 loops on hook) 3 times. 1 loop rem on hook. Do not turn.

3rd row: Forward pass: (Right to left). Tss in each of first 3 sts. Tss in single vertical bar of next Square. 5 loops on hook. Do not turn.

Return pass: (Left to right). (Yoh and draw through 2 loops on hook) 4 times. 1 loop rem on hook. Do not turn.

4th row: Forward pass: (Right to left). Tss in each of first 4 sts. Tss in single vertical bar of next square. 6 loops on hook. Do not turn.

Return pass: (Left to right). (Yoh and draw through 2 loops on hook) 5 times. 1 loop rem on hook. Do not turn.

5th row: Forward pass: (Right to left). Tss in each of first 5 sts. Tss in single vertical bar of next square. 7 loops on hook. Do not turn.

Return pass: (Left to right). (Yoh and draw through 2 loops on hook) 6 times. 1 loop rem on hook. Do not turn.

6th row: Forward pass: Sl st loosely in each of next 5 single vertical bars. Sl st in top of next square. First Triangle of Third Strip is complete.

First to Eighth Squares: With C, work as given for First Square of Second Strip.

Last Triangle

1. 1st row:

Forward pass: (Right to left). Tss in each of first 5 sts. Draw up a loop in same sp were last st was made. 7 loops on hook. Do not turn.

Work from **** to ** as given for last Triangle of First Strip. Fasten off at end of last row.

Keeping cont of Stripe Pat, rep Second and Third Strips for pat until work from beg measures approx 42" [106.5 cm], ending on 3rd Strip. Fasten off.

Lacy Shell Afghan

Approximately 54 x 62 ins.

(For Intermediate Crocheters)

Materials:

Columbia-Minerva Nantuk 4-ply (4 oz. ball)-4 Color A; 3 each of Colors B, C and D.

Nantuk colors shown are (A) Winter White, (B) Lt Iced Jade, (C) Med Iced Jade, (D) Dk Iced Jade.

CROCHET HOOK: Size I-or size needed to obtain gauge given below.

Afghan Crochet Tutorials

GAUGE: Each full shell motif should measure 10 ½ ins. across widest point and 6 ½ ins. from lower point to upper edge.

Take time to check finished size of motif.

FULL SHELL MOTIF: (Make 77 in all - 25 with A, 16 with B, 20 with C and 16 with D.)

Instructions

Row 1: (right side) Beg at point, ch 5 (counts as 1 dc and ch-2 sp), dc in first ch; there are 2 dc with ch-2 sp between. Ch 5, turn.

Row 2: Dc in ch-2 sp, ch 2, dc in 3rd ch of ch-5; there are 3 dc and 2 ch-2 sps. Ch 5, turn.

Row 3: [Dc in ch-2 sp, ch 2] twice, dc in 3rd ch of ch-5; there are 4 dc and 3 ch-2 sps. Ch 5, turn.

Row 4: [Dc in ch-2 sp, ch 2] 3 times, dc in 3rd ch of ch-5; there are 5 dc and 4 ch-2 sps. Ch 3 (counts as 1 dc), turn.

Row 5: Work 5 dc in each ch-2 sp, end with dc in 3rd ch of ch-5; 22 dc in all. Ch 3, turn.

Row 6: Dc in first dc for inc, dc in each dc across, end with 2 dc in 3rd ch of ch-3; 23 dc. Ch 4 (counts as 1 dc and ch-1 sp), turn.

Row 7: Dc in first dc for inc, ch 1, skip 1 dc, * dc in next dc, ch 1, skip 1 dc; rep from * across, end with dc, ch 1, dc all in 3rd ch of ch-3; 14 dc and 13 ch-1 sps. Ch 3, turn.

Afghan Crochet Tutorials

Row 8: Work 2 dc in first ch-1 sp, * dc in next dc, dc in next ch-1 sp, dc in next dc, 2 dc in next ch-1 sp; rep from * across, end with 2 dc in 3rd ch of ch-4; 35 dc. Ch 3, turn.

Row 9-Popcorn Row: (right side) Dc in 2nd dc, * work a popcorn (PC) in next st as follows-work 5 dc all in same st, drop lp of last dc from hook and insert hook in top of 5th dc from end, draw dropped lp through dc and tighten st pushing PC to right side (PC complete), dc in each of next 2 dc; rep from * across working last dc in 3rd ch of ch-3; 11 PC with 2 dc each side. Ch 3, turn.

Row 10: Dc in first dc for inc, dc in next dc, * work 2 dc in next dc, dc in next dc; rep from * across, end with 2 dc in 3rd ch of ch-3; 53 dc. Fasten off leaving a 20" end for sewing.

HALF SHELL MOTIF: (Make 16 in all-8 with B and 8 with D.)

Rows 1- 4: Leaving a 12" end for sewing at beg of point, rep rows 1-4 of full shell motif; 5 dc and 4 ch-2 sps. Ch 3, turn.

Row 5: Work 2 dc in each ch-2 sp across, end with dc in 3rd ch of ch-5; 10 dc in all. Ch 3, turn.

Note: Throughout rem rows of motif, end with last dc(s) of rep in 3rd ch of turning-ch.

Row 6: Dc in first dc for inc, dc in each dc to end; 11 dc. Ch 4, turn.

Row 7: Dc in 3rd dc, * ch 1, skip 1 dc, dc in next dc; rep from * to end; there are 6 dc and 5 ch-1 sps. Ch 3, turn.

Afghan Crochet Tutorials

Row 8: Dc in first dc, * work 2 dc in next ch-1 sp, dc in next dc; rep from * to end; 17 dc in all. Ch 3, turn.

Row 9: Dc in 2nd dc, * work PC in next dc, dc in each of next 2 dc; rep from * to end; 5 PC with 2 dc each side. Ch 3, turn.

Row 10: Dc in first dc, * dc in next dc, 2 dc in next dc; rep from * to end; 26 dc. Fasten off.

JOINING: Follow arrangement chart for placement and color of motifs. Sew motifs tog from the right side using a blunt needle and an overhand st, working through the back lp of each st along top edge of full shells. Use long ends for sewing, working with the darker of the 2 colors to be joined. Secure ends and work in on wrong side after all joining points on each row are completed.

Beg in upper right corner with first 2 rows of full shells. * Mark the center st (27th st) on top edge of one full B shell. Beg at point, sew lower left edge of A shell along top right half of B shell to center st; with same yarn sew lower right edge of next A shell along rem half of B shell; rep from * across row having 5 A shells and 4 B shells.

To join half shells, with top edge of half shell at side edge of afghan, fit upper side edge of half shell along one lower side edge of full shell above; matching rows, sew in place. Stretch lower side edge of half shell along half of top edge of full shell below and sew in place.

Join motifs in same way through next to last row. On last row, reverse full shells and sew lower side edges tog forming scalloped

Afghan Crochet Tutorials

edge. Steam afghan lightly on wrong side and pat into shape.

ARRANGEMENT CHART

Crochet One to Two Skein Throw

Crochet HookK/10.5 or 6.5 mm hook

Yarn Weight(4) Medium Weight/Worsted Weight and Aran (16-20 stitches to 4 inches)

Crochet Gauge2 repeats = 7-1/2"; 6 rows = 4" in pat. CHECK YOUR GAUGE. Use any size hook to obtain the gauge.

Afghan Crochet Tutorials

Finished Size 35" x 42"

Materials

RED HEART® "Super Saver® Jumbo": 2 skeins* 631 Light Sage

*Note: The size used to be larger which is why only one skein was needed. One skein of a similar yarn may be substituted.

Crochet Hook: 6.5mm [US K-10.5]

Yarn needle

Find other easy crochet patterns inside our collection of How Do I Crochet? 13 Basic Crochet Stitches and Free Beginner Crochet Afghan Patterns free eBook

How Do I Crochet? 13 Basic Crochet Stitches and Free Beginner Crochet Afghan Patterns free eBook

Instructions:

Ch 121.

Row 1 (Wrong Side): Sc in 2nd ch from hook and in next 2 ch, * ch 3, skip next 3 ch, sc in next ch, ch 3, skip next 2 ch, sc in next ch, ch 3, skip next 3 ch, sc in next 3 ch; rep from * across; turn.

Row 2 (Right Side): Ch 4, skip first sc, 3 tr in next sc, skip next ch-3 sp; (2trcl, ch 3, 2trcl, ch 3, 2trcl) all in next ch-3 sp – tr shell made; skip next ch-3 sp, * 5 tr in center sc of next 3-sc group, skip next ch-3 sp, tr shell in next ch-3 sp, skip next ch-3 sp; rep from * to last 3 sc;

Afghan Crochet Tutorials

skip next sc, 3 tr in next sc, tr in last sc; turn.

Row 3: Ch 1, sc in next 3 tr, * skip next tr, [ch 3, sc in next ch-3 sp] twice, ch 3, skip next tr, sc in next 3 tr, rep from * across working last sc in top of ch-4; turn. Rep Rows 2 and 3 twenty-six more times, then rep Row 2 once more.

Last Row: Ch 1, sc in first 3 tr, * skip next tr, ch 3, sc in next ch-3 sp, ch 2, sc in next ch-3 sp, ch 3, skip next tr, sc in next 3 tr; rep from * across working last sc in top of ch-4; turn.

Do not fasten off but work Edging as follows:

Edging-Rnd 1: Ch 1, * (sc, ch 1, sc) all in first sc, sc in next 2 sc, ** 2 sc in ch-3 sp, sc in next sc, sc in ch-2 sp, sc in next sc, 2 sc in ch-3 sp ***, sc in next 3 sc; rep from ** to last 3 sc, end at ***; sc in next 2 sc, (sc, ch 1, sc) all in last sc; turn to work down side edge; **** work 3 sc over tr at edge, sc in st at end of next row; rep from **** to next corner st; turn to work across bottom edge; work in same manner across bottom and then next side edge; join with a sl st in first sc; turn.

Rnd 2: Ch 1, sc in each sc around and work (sc, ch 1, sc) in each corner ch-1 sp; join. Fasten off.

Abbreviations

(SPECIAL) 2trcl * [yo] twice, draw up a loop in st, [yo and draw through 2 loops on hook] twice; rep from * once more; yo and draw through all 3 loops on hook.

Afghan Crochet Tutorials

Arrow Stitch Afghan

Crochet HookH/8 or 5 mm hook

Yarn Weight(4) Medium Weight/Worsted Weight and Aran (16-20 stitches to 4 inches)

Materials:

10 balls Bernat Berella yarn in Rose (MC)

Afghan Crochet Tutorials

5 balls Bernat Berella yarn in Natural (A)

Size 5 mm (U.S. H or 8) crochet hook, or size needed to obtain gauge

Gauge: 13 sts and 10 rows = 4 ins 10 cm in pat.

If you like this pattern, be sure to take a look at Crochet Through the Years: Vintage Crochet Afghan Patterns.

Instructions:

Finished Size Approx 51 x 62 ins 129.5 x 157.5 cm

With A ch 201.

1st row: (RS). 1 sc in 2nd ch from hook. 1 sc in each ch to end of ch. Ch 1. Turn. 200 sts.

2nd row: 1 sc in first sc and each sc to end of row. Join MC. Ch 3. Turn.

3rd row: Miss first st. 1 dc in next st. Miss next 3 sts. 1 tr in next st. Working behind tr just made, 1 dc in first missed st. 1 dc in each of next 2 missed sts. Miss next 3 sts after tr. 1 tr in next st. Working behind tr just made, 1 dc in first missed st. 1 dc in each of next 2 missed sts. Rep from to last 2 sts. 1 dc in each of last 2 sts. Ch 3. Turn.

4th row: Miss first st. 1 dc in next dc. Miss next 3 dc. 1 tr in next tr. Working in front of tr just made, 1 dc in first missed dc. 1 dc in each of next 2 missed dc. Miss next 3 dc after tr. 1 tr in next tr. Working in

Afghan Crochet Tutorials

front of tr just made, 1 dc in first missed dc. 1 dc in each of next 2 missed dc. Rep from to last 2 sts. 1 dc in each of last 2 sts. Join A. Ch 1. Turn.

5th row: 1 sc in first st and each st to end of row. Ch 1. Turn.

Rows 2 to 5 inclusive form pat.

Cont in pat until work from beg measures approx 50 ins 127 cm ending on a 2nd row of pat and omitting turning ch at end of last row.

Fasten off. Edging: Join MC to any corner of afghan and work 1 row sc evenly around outer edge, working 3 sc in corners. Join with ss to first sc.

Next rnd: Working reverse sc from left to right instead of from right to left as usual, work 1 sc in each sc around outer edge of Afghan. Ss to first sc. Fasten off.

Ferris Wheel Baby Blanket

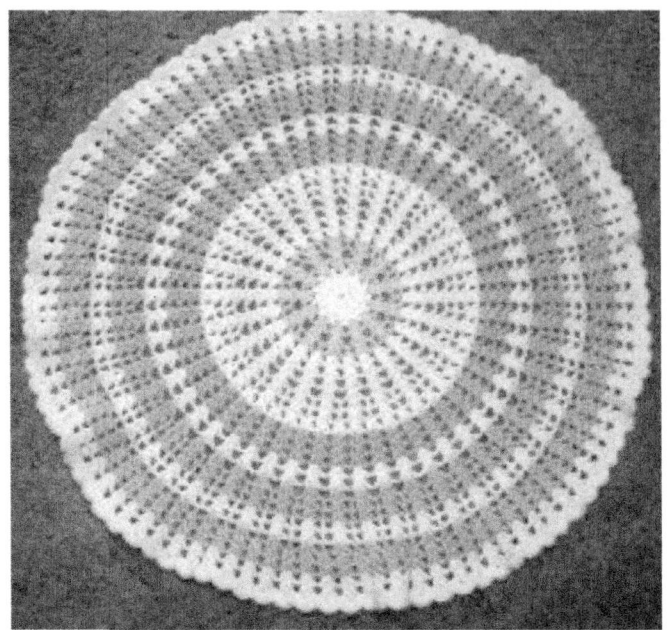

Materials:

- 12 oz. 4-ply worsted weight acrylic total (I had forgotten to weigh each color - this is why the pattern is written without color changes)

- J hook

Size: 32" across

Notes:

- this pattern is written without the color changes

Afghan Crochet Tutorials

- this blanket is a little ruffley towards the end

- the ch 2 at the beginning of Rnds 1 & 2 do not count as a stitch

Instructions:

Rnd 1: Ch 3, 13 dc in 3rd ch from hook. Join with a sl st to 1st dc. (13 dc)

Rnd 2: Ch 2, 2 dc in each dc around. Join as before. (26 dc)

Rnd 3: Ch 1, sc in same st, ch 3. *skip next dc, sc in next dc, ch 3. Repeat from * around. Join with a sl st to 1st sc.

Rnd 4: Sl st into ch-3 space, (ch 3, 2 dc) in same space, ch 1. (3 dc, ch 1) in each ch-3 space around. Join with a sl st to top of beginning ch 3.

Rnd 5: Sl st into next dc, (ch 3, 2 dc) in same dc, ch 2. (3 dc, ch 2) in middle dc of each 3 dc cluster around. Join as before.

Rnd 6: Sl st into next dc, (ch 3, 2 dc) in same dc, ch 1, dc in ch-2 space, ch 1. *3 dc in middle dc of next 3 dc cluster, ch 1, dc in ch-2 space, ch 1. Repeat from * around. Join as before.

Rnd 7: Sl st into next dc, (ch 3, 2 dc) in same dc, ch 1, 3 dc in next dc, ch 1. *3 dc in middle dc of next 3 dc cluster, ch 1, 3 dc in next dc, ch 1. Repeat from * around. Join as before.

Rnd 8: Sl st into next dc, (ch 3, 2 dc) in same dc, ch 1. (3 dc, ch 1) in middle dc of each 3 dc cluster around. Join as before.

Rnds 9 - 10: Repeat Rnd 5.

Rnd 11: Repeat Rnd 6.

Rnd 12: Sl st into next dc, (ch 3, 2 dc) in same dc, ch 1, dc in next dc, ch 1. *3 dc in middle dc of next 3 dc cluster, ch 1, dc in next dc, ch 1. Repeat from * around. Join as before.

Rnd 13: Repeat Rnd 7.

Rnds 14 - 17: Repeat Rnd 8.

Rnds 18 - 19: Repeat Rnd 5.

Rnd 20: Repeat Rnd 6.

Rnds 21 - 24: Repeat Rnd 12.

Rnd 25: Repeat Rnd 7.

Rnds 26 - 28: Repeat Rnd 8.

Rnd 29: Ch 1, sc in same st, sc in each dc and ch-1 space around. Join with a sl st to 1st sc.

Rnd 30: Sl st into next sc, (ch 3, 3 dc) in same sc, skip next sc, sc in next sc, skip next sc. *4 dc in next sc, skip next sc, sc in next sc, skip next sc. Repeat from * around. Join with a sl st to top of beginning ch 3. End off.

Crocheted Cuddly Kittens Afghan

Size 38" by 44' before fringing

Materials: knitting weight worsted yarn:

Afghan Crochet Tutorials

16 oz White

12 oz Baby Blue

8 oz True Blue

Size H aluminum crochet hook (or size required for gauge)

Gauge

5 Shells = 7"

Gauge Note: Each shell = (2 dc, ch 1, 2 dc).

Instructions

With Baby Blue, ch 139 loosely.

Row 1 (right side): Dc in 4th ch from hook. Dc in next ch sk 2 chs, work beg shell over next 2 chs as follows: 2 Dc in next ch, ch 1, 2 Dc in next ch (beg shell made). * Sk 3 chs, work beg shell over next 2 chs (as before); rep from * to last 5 chs; sk 2 chs, Dc in each of last 3 chs = 26 shells.

Row 2: Ch 3, turn; Dc in each of next 2 Dc, * work (2 Dc, ch 1, 2 Dc) in ch-1 sp of next shell (shell made); rep from * to last 2 Dc, dc in each of last 2 dc; dc in top of ch-3, changing to White. (TO Change colors: Work dc until 2 lps rem on hook, finish off color being used, leave approx 4" end for weaving in now or later. With new color (leave approx 4" end) YO and draw through 2 lps on hook = color changed.)

Afghan Crochet Tutorials

Row 3: With white, ch 3, turn; dc in each of next 2 dc, work puff st (abbreviated PS) in sp before first shell in 2nd Row below as follows; Work (YO and insert hook in space before first shell in 2nd Row below (1. Hook yarn and draw up a long loop to height of working Row) 4 times. (9 loops now on hook. 2. YO and draw through first 8 loops on hook then YO and draw through rem 2 loops on hook = PS made. * Work a shell in ch-1 sp of each shell (in working Row), Work PS in next SP between Shells in 2nd Row below; rep

from * to last shell; work a shell in ch-1 sp of last shell, work PS in sp after last shell in 2nd Row below; dc in each of last 2dc (in working Row), dc in top of ch-3 = 27 PS.

Row 4: Ch 3, turn; dc in each of next 2 dc, * sk PS, work shell in

Ch-1 sp of next shell; rep from * to last PS; sk last PS, dc in each of last 2 dc, dc in top of ch-3 = 26 shells.

Row 5: Rep Row 2, changing to True Blue in last dc.

Rows 6 and 7: With True blue, rep rows 3 and 4.

ROW 8: With True Blue, rep Row 2, changing to white in last dc.

ROM 9 and 10: With white, rep Rows 3 and 4.

Row 11: With White, rep Row2, changing to Baby Blue in last dc.

Rows 12 and 13: With Baby Blue rep Rows 3 and 4.

Row 14: With Baby Blue, rep Row 2, changing to white in last dc.

Afghan Crochet Tutorials

Rep Rows 3 through 14, 4 times more; then rep rows 3 through 13 once more. (You should now have 2 rows of Baby Blue at top edge)

Finish off and weave in all ends.

FRINGE Both short edges. Cut 12' strands of Baby Blue. (Or color of your choice) Use 2 strands for each knot. Tie one knot in every Other st across edge.

Princess Crocodile Stitch Baby Blanket

Crochet HookI/9 or 5.5 mm hook

Yarn Weight(3) Light/DK (21-24 stitches to 4 inches)

Crochet Gauge6 V-sts and 8 rows = 4" [10 cm]

Afghan Crochet Tutorials

Finished SizeApprox 35" [89 cm] square

Materials

Bernat® Softee Baby™ (140 g/5 oz; 331 m/362 yds) - Mint (02004) 7 balls

Size 5.5 mm (U.S. I or 9) crochet hook or size needed to obtain gauge

Optional: 7 yds [6.5 m] of contrast color satin ribbon 3/8" [9 mm] wide

The crochet crocodile stitch has never been accused of being boring. With exciting texture and unique design, crocodile stitch patterns have so much personality, they seem to leap out at you.You'll find some of the coolest patterns in Crazy for the Crochet Crocodile Stitch: 4 Crocodile Stitch Patterns

Crazy for the Crochet Crocodile Stitch: 4 Crocodile Stitch Patterns

Instructions

Instructions for BLANKET:

NOTES:

The "crocodile stitch" is formed by a 2 row repeat: a row of V-sts followed by a row of scales (or shells). This is a fairly easy pattern to execute and fast to memorize. The novelty of this design is that the scales are crocheted in front of the V-sts with clusters of double crochet (dc) from top to bottom, then from bottom to top, as opposed to working them on top of the row, like in most shell patterns.

Ch 3 at beg of rnd counts as dc throughout.

Ch 124.

1st row: (WS). (1 dc. Ch 1. 1 dc) in 7th ch from hook (counts as 1 dc. Ch 1. 1 dc. Ch 1. 1 dc). *Miss next 2 ch. (1 dc. Ch 1. 1 dc) in next ch - V-st made. Rep from * to last 3 ch. Miss next 2 ch. 1 dc in last ch. Turn. 39 V-sts.

2nd row: Ch 3. Work 4 dc down post of first dc of first V-st. Ch 1. Work 5 dc up post of 2nd dc of the same V-st - beg scale st made (see photo step 1 below). *Miss next V-st. Work 5 dc down post of first dc of next V-st. Ch 1. Work 5 dc up post of 2nd dc of the same V-st - scale st made. Rep from * to last dc. Sl st in last dc. Turn. 20 scale sts (see photo step 2 below).

3rd row: Ch 3. V-st in first ch-1 sp of 1st row. *Inserting hook from front to back between next 2 scales and ch-1 sp of 1st row directly behind it, work V-st (see photo step 3 below). Rep from * to last dc. 1 dc in top of last dc of 1st row. Turn. 39 V-sts (see photo step 4 below).

4th row: Sl st in each of first 2 dc and next ch-1 sp. Miss next dc. *Scale st around next V-st. Miss next V-st. Rep from * to last V-st. Miss next dc. Sl st in next ch-1 sp and each of last 2 dc. Turn. 19

Afghan Crochet Tutorials

scale sts.

5th row: Ch 3. V-st in first ch-1 sp. *V-st in next ch-1 sp. Inserting hook from front to back between next 2 scales and ch-1 sp of 3rd row directly behind it, work V-st. Rep from * to last ch-1 sp. V-st in last ch-1 sp. 1 dc in last dc. Turn. 39 V-sts.

6th row: Ch 1. Scale st around first V-st. *Miss next V-st. Scale st around next V-st. Rep from * to last dc. Sl st in last dc. Turn. 20 scale sts. Rep 3rd to 6th rows 21 times more, ending on a 6th row. Do not break yarn. There will be 45 rows of scales.

Instructions for EDGING:

1st rnd: (RS). Ch 1. 2 sc in same sp as last sl st. Work 89 sc down left side of Blanket, 3 sc in corner, 119 sc across bottom of Blanket, 3 sc in corner, 89 sc up right side of Blanket, 119 sc across top of Blanket and 1 sc in same sp as first sc. Join with sl st in top of first sc. 428 sc.

2nd rnd: Ch 6 (counts as dc and ch-3). 1 dc in same sp as sl st. *[Ch 1. Miss next sc. 1 dc in next sc. Ch 1. Rep from * to next corner sc, (1 dc. Ch 3. 1 dc) in next corner sc] 3 times. **Ch 1. Miss next sc. 1 dc in next sc. Ch 1. Rep from ** to next corner sc. Join with sl st in 3rd ch of ch 6.

3rd rnd: Sl st in first ch-3 sp. Ch 3. 4 dc in same sp as last sl st. *3 dc in each ch-1 sp to next ch- 3 sp. 5 dc in next ch-3 sp. Rep from * around, ending with 3 dc in each ch-1 sp to next ch-3 sp. Join with sl st in top of ch 3.

Afghan Crochet Tutorials

4th rnd: Ch 3. 2 dc in each dc around. Join with sl st in top of ch 3.

5th rnd: Ch 3. *2 dc in next dc. 1 dc in next dc. Rep from * around. Join with sl st in top of ch 3. Fasten off.

Instructions for FINISHING:

Optional: Cut 4 pieces of ribbon measuring 60" [152 cm] each. Weave one ribbon piece along each edge of Blanket. Tie bows at each corner.

Rainbow Delight Baby Afghan

Materials: Worsted Weight Yarn 24 ozs Pastel Variegated

Aluminum Crochet Hook Size J or 6.00 mm

Finished Size Approximately 37" x 54"

Gauge: 4 rows in pattern = 2"

Instructions

Afghan:

Beginning at one end, ch 131.

Afghan Crochet Tutorials

Row 1: Sc in 4th ch from hook, * ch 1, sk 1 ch, sc in next ch. Rep from *across, ch 2, turn. (64 ch-1 sps)

Row 2: * Sk 1 ch-1 sp, hdc n next ch-1 sp, hdc in skipped ch-1 sp. Repfrom * across, hdc in top of turning ch-2, ch 3, turn. (32 cross sts)

Row 3: * 4 dc in center between each hdc of each cross st. Rep from *across, dc in top of ch-3 turning ch, ch 1, turn. (32--4 dc shells)

Row 4: Sc in first dc, * ch 1, sk 1 dc, sc in next dc. Rep from * across, ch2, turn.

Row 5: * Sk ch-1 sp, sc in next sc, ch 1. Rep from * across, sc in turningch-2 sp, ch 2, turn.

Repeat rows 2-5 until piece measures 53" from beginning.

Next Row: Rep row 2, ch 2, turn at end of row.

Next Row: * Sk 1 st, sc in next st. Rep from * across. Break off.

Finishing:

Fringe: Cut 13" lengths of yarn. Fold 4 lengths in half and knot in each

ch-1 sp at both ends of afghan. Trim ends evenly.

The Coziest Crocheted Baby Blanket Ever

Crochet HookL/11 or 8 mm hook

Yarn Weight(5) Bulky/Chunky (12-15 stitches for 4 inches)

Afghan Crochet Tutorials

Crochet Gauge8 dc = 4"; 5 rows = 4"

Finished Size30 x 32 inches

Materials

Red Heart Buttercup: #4273 Light Yellow Multi (8 balls)

US size L/11 (8.0 mm) hook

Yarn needle

Instructions

Blanket

Ch 61.

Row 1: Double crochet in 2nd chain from hook and each chain across. (60 double crochet)

Row 2: Chain 2 (counts as double crochet), turn, working in front loops only, double crochet in each double crochet across.

Rows 3-41: Repeat Row 2. Fasten off.

Rose Twists Afghan

Materials:

Yarn: Lily Sugar 'n Cream Twists (56.7 g/2 oz) 6 balls of #20420 (Rose Twists) as MC

Lily Sugar 'n Cream (70.9 g/ 2.5 oz) 6 balls of #01004 (Soft Ecru) as A

Crochet Hook: Size 5 mm (U.S. H or 8) crochet hook or size needed to obtain gauge

Afghan Crochet Tutorials

Diagram

Size: Approx 40½ ins [103 cm] wide x 48½ ins [123 cm] long.

Gauge: Motif = 8 ins [20.5 cm] square.

Instructions:

Motif A (make 15).

With MC, ch 5. Join with sl st to form a ring.

1st rnd: Ch 3 (counts as dc). 3 dc. (Ch 3. 4 dc) 3 times in ring. Ch 3. Join with sl st to top of ch 3.

2nd rnd: Ch 3 (counts as dc). 1 dc in each of next 3 dc. (2 dc. Ch 3. 2 dc) in next ch-3 sp. *1 dc in each of next 4 dc. (2 dc. Ch 3. 2 dc) in next ch-3 sp. Rep from * twice more. Join with sl st to top of ch 3.

3rd to 7th rnds: Ch 3 (counts as dc). *1 dc in each dc to next ch-3 sp. (2 dc. Ch 3. 2 dc) in next ch-3 sp. Rep from * 3 times more. 1 dc in each dc to end of rnd. Join with sl st to top of ch 3. Fasten off.

Motif B (make 15).

With A, work as given for Motif A.

Finishing

Crochet motifs tog as shown in diagram below.

Edging

1st rnd: Join MC with sl st to any corner of Blanket. Work 1 row of

Afghan Crochet Tutorials

sc evenly around, having 3 sc in corner ch-3 sps. Join with sl st to first sc.

2nd rnd: Ch 1. Work 1 row of sc evenly around having 3 sc in corner sc. Join with sl st to first sc. Fasten off.

Snowflake Afghan

Materials: 32 oz. dark, 28 oz. light worsted-weight yarn. G hook (4.25 mm)

Stitches: U.S. terminology

Hexagon (make 59)

Instructions:

Rnd 1: With light color ch 2, 6 sc in second chain from hook, sl st in beg sc.

Afghan Crochet Tutorials

Rnd 2: Ch 5 (counts as dc and ch 2), dc in first sc, *(dc, ch 2, dc) in next sc, repeat from * 4 times; sl st in 3rd ch of ch-5.

Rnd 3: Sl st to ch-2 sp, ch 3 (counts as first dc on this and following rnds), (dc, ch 3, 2 dc) in first ch-2 sp, *(2 dc, ch 3, 2 dc) in next ch-2 sp, repeat from * 4 times; sl st in top of ch-3.

Rnd 4: Sl st in each st to ch-3 sp, (ch 3, 2 dc, ch 3, 3 dc, ch 1) in first ch-3 sp, *(3 dc, ch 3, 3 dc, ch 1) in next ch-3 sp, repeat from * 4 times; sl st in top of ch-3.

Rnd 5: Sl st in each st to ch-3 sp, (ch 3, 3 dc, ch 2, 4 dc, ch 3) in first ch-3 sp, *(4 dc, ch 2, 4 dc, ch 3) in next ch-3 sp, repeat from * 4 times; sl st in top of ch-3. Cut yarn and fasten. [6 pointed snowflake]

Rnd 6: Join dark colored yarn by making a slip knot on hook and joining with an sc in ch-2 sp, (ch 1, sc) in same sp, *working in sps between dc, hdc in each of next 2 sps, dc in next sp, 2 dc in next ch-3 sp, trc in ch-1 sp on rnd 4 (below), 2 dc in same ch-3 sp on rnd 5, dc in next sp (between dc), hdc in each of next 2 sps, (sc, ch 1, sc) in next ch-2 sp, repeat from * 4 times; working in sps between dc, hdc in each of next 2 sps, dc in next sp, 2 dc in next ch-3 sp, trc in ch-1 sp on rnd 4 (below), 2 dc in same ch-3 sp on rnd 5, dc in next sp (between dc), hdc in each of next 2 sps, sl st in beg sc.

Rnd 7: Ch 3 (first dc), *(dc, ch 3, dc) in ch-1 sp, dc in each of next 13 sts, repeat from * 4 times; (dc, ch 3, dc) in last ch-1 sp, dc in each of next 12 sts, sl st in top of ch-3.

Afghan Crochet Tutorials

Rnd 8: Ch 1, sc in first st, sc in next st, *3 sc in ch-3 sp, sc in each of next 15 sts, repeat from * 4 times; 3 sc in last ch-3 sp, sc in each of next 13 sts, sl st in beg sc. Cut yarn and fasten.

Assembly

Using dark color, whipstitch hexagons together forming 5 strips of 7 hexagons each and 4 strips of 6 hexagons each. Whipstitch strips together (7,6,7,6,7,6,7,6,7).

Edging

Row 1: With right side facing join light color with an sc, sc in each st around; sl st in beg sc, ch 1 and turn.

Row 2: Sc in first st, *trc in next st, sc in next st, repeat from * around; sl st in beg sc. Cut yarn and fasten.

Finishing: Weave in all loose ends

Shades of Amber Tunisian Afghan

Crochet Hook J/10 or 6 mm hook

Yarn Weight(4) Medium Weight/Worsted Weight and Aran (16-20 stitches to 4 inches)

Afghan Crochet Tutorials

Crochet Gauge 14-1/2 sts and 16 rows = 4" [10 cm] in pat.

Finished Size Approx 42" x 56" [106.5 x 142 cm]

Materials

Bernat® Super Value™ (Solids: 197 g/7 oz; 389 m/426 yds; Ombres: 142 g/5 oz; 251 m/275 yds); Contrast A (53241 Moss Heather) 1 ball; Contrast B (28244 Hiking Ombre) 1 ball; Contrast C (53246 Lush) 1 ball; Contrast D (28822 Summerset Ombre) 3 balls; Contrast E (53531 Rouge) 1 ball; Contrast F (28101 Wild Flowers Ombre) 3 balls; Contrast G (53609 Bronze) 1 ball

Size 6 mm (U.S. J or 10) Tunisian crochet hook

Size 6 mm (U.S. J or 10) crochet hook or size needed to obtain gauge

Instructions:

1ST SQUARE:

With A and Tunisian hook, ch 24.

1. 1st row: (Row from right to left). Draw up a loop in 2nd ch from hook. Draw up a loop and leave on hook in each rem ch to end of chain. 23 loops.

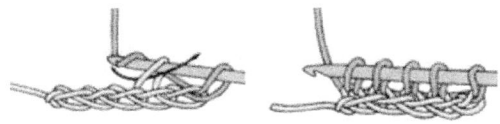

Afghan Crochet Tutorials

2. **2nd row: (Row from left to right). Draw yarn through only last loop (edge st). *Draw yarn through 2 loops. Rep from * until 1 loop rem on hook. Do not turn.

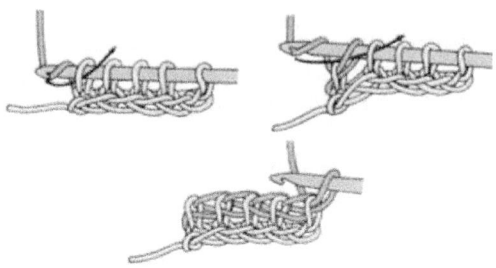

3. 3rd row: (Row from right to left). *Insert hook from right to left behind single vertical thread. Draw up a loop and leave on hook. Rep from * to end of row.

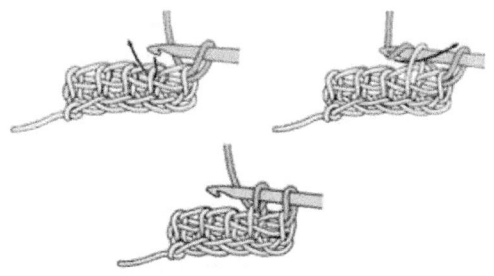

4. 4th row: (Row from left to right). Draw yarn through only last loop (edge st). *Draw yarn through 2 loops. Rep from * until 1 loop rem on hook. Do not turn. Rep last 2 rows until work from beg measures approx 6-3/4" [17 cm], ending with 4th (return) row.

Fasten off.**

2ND SQUARE:

1st row: (Pick up forward row). With RS facing and Tunisian hook, draw up B through first side st, working through 2 loops of side sts, draw up 22 more loops evenly across side edge. 23 loops total. Work from ** to ** as given for 1st Square.

3RD SQUARE:

With C, work as for 2nd Square.

4TH SQUARE:

With B, work as for 2nd Square. Following diagrams, cont in same manner until all Squares are complete.

EDGING:

1st rnd: With standard crochet hook and RS facing, join A with sl st to top corner of Blanket. Ch 1. 2 sc in same sp as last sl st. *18 sc across first Square. (19 sc across next Square) 4 times. 18 sc across next Square. 3 sc in corner. 18 sc across first Square. (19 sc across next Square) 6 times. 18 sc across next Square.** 3 sc in corner. Rep from * to ** once more. 1 sc in same sp as first 2 sc. Join with sl st to first sc.

2nd rnd: Ch 1. 2 sc in same sp as last sl st. 1 sc in each sc around, having 3 sc in corner sc. 1 sc in same sp as first sc. Join F with sl st to first sc.

Afghan Crochet Tutorials

3rd rnd: With F, ch 1. (1 sc. Ch 2. 1 sc) in same sp as last sl st. [*Ch 1. Miss next sc. 1 sc in next sc. Rep from * to 1 sc before corner sc. Ch 1. Miss next sc. (1 sc. Ch 2. 1 sc) in corner sc] 3 times. **Ch 1. Miss next sc. 1 sc in next sc. Rep from ** to last sc. Ch 1. Miss last sc. Join A with sl st to first sc.

4th rnd: With A, sl st to next ch-2 sp. Ch 1. 2 sc in same sp as last sl st. [*1 sc in missed sc of 2nd row over ch-1 sp. 1 sc in next sc. Rep from * to corner ch-2 sp. 3 sc in corner ch-2 sp] 3 times. **1 sc in missed sc of 2nd row over ch-1 sp. 1 sc in next sc. Rep from ** around, ending with 1 sc in same sp as first sc. Join with sl st to first sc.

5th rnd: As 2nd rnd. Join D with sl st to first sc.

6th rnd: With D, ch 1. Working from left to right instead of right to left as usual, work 1 reverse sc in each sc around. Join with sl st to first sc.

Fasten off.

Afghan Crochet Tutorials

White Hibiscus Hexagon Afghan

Materials

How to Bind Off Knitting with a Crochet Hook – Video and Photo Tutorial

3 colors worsted weight yarn

H hook

tapestry needle, scissors

Afghan Crochet Tutorials

Resources and tutorials you may find helpful in following this pattern: Crochet Abbreviations, U.S. to U.K. Crochet Conversion Chart, How to Make a Magic Ring, Crochet Stitch Chart Symbols.

Instructions:

Special Stitches:

Long single crochet (Lsc): Insert hook in designated space and pull up a loop to height of row being worked, complete as single crochet.

With CA, make a magic ring.

Round 1: Ch 3 (counts as 1st dc), work 1 dc in ring, ch 1, *2 dc in ring, ch 1, rep from * 4 more times, join in top of beg ch 3, fasten off — 12 dc and 6 ch-1 sps.

Round 2: Join CB in any ch-1 sp, ch 3 (counts as 1st dc), work [1 dc, ch 5, 2 dc] in same ch-sp as color was joined, *ch 1, [2 dc, ch 5, 2 dc] in next ch-1 sp, rep from * 4 more times, ch 1, join in top of beg ch 3 — 24 dc and 6 ch-5 sps.

Round 3: Sl st in next dc and in next ch-5 sp, ch 3 (counts as 1st dc), work 6 dc in same ch-sp, *ch 1, work 7 dc in next ch-5 sp, rep from * rep from * 4 more times, ch 1, join in top of beg ch 3, fasten off — 42 dc and 6 ch-1 sps.

Here is where I stopped for this project. To continue on with the traditional hexagon shaped African Flower motif scroll to the bottom of the page for the last 2 rounds.

Afghan Crochet Tutorials

JOINING

To join, I used the Join As You Go Method (JAYGO) as follows:

For the first motif only, join CC in the first dc of any 7 dc-grouping from Round 3, ch 1 (does not count as st), work 1 sc in same st as color was joined and in next 6 sts, *work 1 Lsc over the ch-1 sp from Round 3 and into the ch-1 sp from Round 2, work 1 sc in each of the next 7 sts, rep from * 4 more times, work 1 Lsc into the ch-1 sp from Round 2, join in first st of round, fasten off — 48 sts.

For subsequent motifs, follow the same pattern as for the first, but when you reach the side to join, after working your Lsc, work 1 sc in each of the next 3 sts, ch 1, then drop the loop from your hook and insert it into the 4th sc of the motif you want to join it to, put the loop back on your hook and pull it through, now continuing to work back in your current motif, work 1 sc in each of the next 4 sts. Repeat this for the next petal of your motif.

Each motif should join to another at 2 points. See the diagram below for placement of the motifs. Joining points are indicated by the red diamonds.

To make the traditional hexagon African Flower motif, follow Rounds 1 through 3 above and then continue on as follows:

Round 4: Join CC in the first dc of any 7 dc-grouping from Round 3, ch 1 (does not count as st), work 1 sc in same st as color was joined and in next 6 sts, *work 1 Lsc over the ch-1 sp from Round 3 and

Afghan Crochet Tutorials

into the ch-1 sp from Round 2, work 1 sc in each of the next 7 sts, rep from * 4 more times, work 1 Lsc into the ch-1 sp from Round 2, join in first st of round, fasten off — 48 sts.

Round 5: Join CD in same st, ch 3 (counts as 1st dc), work 1 dc in each of the next 2 sts, *[1 dc, ch 1, 1 dc] in next st, 1 dc in each of the next 7 sts, rep from * 4 more times, [1 dc, ch 1, 1 dc] in next st, 1 dc in each of the next 4 sts, join in top of beg ch-3, fasten off — 54 sts.

Blue Heirloom Afghan

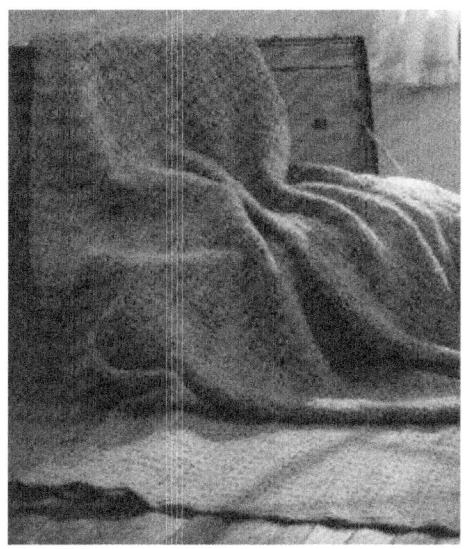

Materials: Worsted Weight Yarn 3

Crochet Hook Size I or 5.50 mm

Approximate Finished Size 58 x 72

Ch 257.

Instructions:

Row 1: Dc in 4th ch from hook; dc in next 6 ch, * sk next 2 ch, in next ch work 3 dc, ch 2, 3 dc;shell made; sk next 2 ch, dc in next 8 ch; rep from * across. Ch 3, turn.

Afghan Crochet Tutorials

Row 2: Skip first st, dc in front lp of next 7 dc, * work shell in ch-2 sp of shell, dc in front lp of next 8 dc;

rep from * across, working last dc in top of turning ch. Ch 3, turn.

Repeat row 2 until piece measures approximately 72 inches, omit ch 3 at end of last row; do not turn.

Border: With right side facing, ch 2, work 2 sc in last dc for corner, work sc evenly spaced along side

of afghan to next corner, work 3 sc in corner, sc in each st across bottom of afghan; work 3 sc in

corner, work sc evenly spaced along side of afghan to next corner, work 3 sc in corner, work hdc in

back lp of each st across top of afghan, join with sl st to first ch. Fasten off.

Colonial Charm Afghan

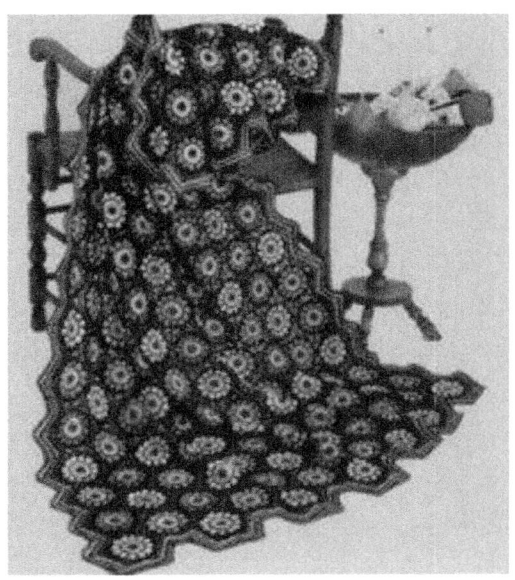

Materials:

CHADWICK'S RED HEART SOCK AND SWEATER YARN, 3 Ply, Shrink-and-Stretch Resist Finish, Art. E.255: 9 skeins (1 oz. "Tangle-Proof" Pull-Out Skeins) of No. 12 Black; 7 skeins of No. 686 Paddy Green; 5 skeins of No. 230 Yellow and 7 skeins of assorted colors.

Clark's O.N.T. Plastic Crochet Hook No. 4.

GAUGE: Each motif measures 4 inches from point to point.

Afghan Crochet Tutorials

Instructions:

FIRST MOTIF . . . Starting at center with Black, ch 5. Join with sl st to form ring. 1st rnd: 12 sc in ring. Join and break off. 2nd rnd: Attach Yellow to first sc, ch 3, dc in same sc, 2 dc in each sc around. Join and break off. 3rd rnd: Attach Black to same place as sl st, sc in same place, sc in back loop of each dc around. Join and break off. 4th rnd: Attach any color of assorted colors to first sc, sc in same place, * sl st in next sc, ch 3, (yarn over, insert hook in same sc, draw loop through) 3 times; yarn over and draw through all loops on hook (puff st made), ch 3, sl st in same sc, sc in next sc. Repeat from * around. Join and break off. 5th rnd: Attach Black to ch-3 preceding any puff st, sc in same place, * ch 3, sc in next ch 3, ch 1, dc in next sc, ch 1, sc in next ch 3. Repeat from * around. Join and break off. 6th rnd: Attach Paddy Green to any dc, sc in same place, * ch 3, sc in next ch-3 loop, ch 3, in next dc make dc, ch 3 and dc; ch 3, sc in next ch-3 loop, ch 3, sc in next dc. Repeat from * around. Join and break off.

SECOND MOTIF . . . Work as for First Motif until 5 rnds have been completed. 6th rnd: Attach Paddy Green to any dc, sc in same place, ch 3, sc in next ch-3 loop, ch 3, dc in next dc, ch 1, sl st in corresponding loop on First Motif, ch 1, dc in same dc on Second Motif, ch 3, sc in next ch-3 loop, ch 1, sl st in corresponding loop on First Motif, ch 1, sc in next dc on Second Motif, ch 1, sl st in next loop on First Motif, ch 1, sc in next ch-3 loop on Second Motif, ch 3, dc in next dc and join next corner loop as before. Complete rnd (no more joinings).

Afghan Crochet Tutorials

Make 13 rows of 16 Motifs, joining adjacent sides as shown on chart as Second Motif was joined to First Motif (where 3 corners meet, join 3rd corner to joining of previous 2 corners).

EDGING . . . 1st rnd: Attach Paddy Green to corner sp of any side motif, ch 3, in same sp make dc, ch 3 and 2 dc; * 3 dc in each of next 4 sps, holding back on hook the last loop of each dc make a dc in next 2 joined loops, thread over and draw through all loops on hook (joint-dc made), 3 dc in each of next 4 sps, in next sp make 2 dc, ch 2 and 2 dc. Repeat from * around, making joint-dc over each joining and 2 dc, ch 3 and 2 dc in each corner loop. Join and break off. 2nd rnd: Attach Yellow to same place as sl st, sc in back loop of next dc, sc in next 3 ch, * sc in back loop of each dc to within 1 dc of next joint-dc, holding back on hook the last loop of each sc make sc in next dc, skip next joint-dc, sc in next dc, thread over and draw through all loops on hook (1 sc decreased). Repeat from * around, decreasing 1 sc over each joint-dc and making sc in each ch of ch-3. Join and break off. 3rd rnd: Attach Black to same place as sl st, sc in same place, sc in back loop of next 2 sc, 3 sc in back loop of next sc, sc in back loop of each sc around, decreasing 1 sc over previous decreases as before and making 3 sc in center sc of each point. Join and break off. 4th rnd: Attach Yellow and repeat last rnd. 5th rnd: Attach Green to same place as sl st, ch 3, dc in back loop of each sc around, making 3 dc in center sc of each point and decreasing 1 dc over previous decreases as before. Join and break off. Block to measurements.

Printed in Great Britain
by Amazon